Making Music with Magnets

Kristina Mercedes Urquhart, M.A.

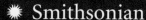 Smithsonian

Contributing Author

Allison Duarte

Consultants

Roger Sherman
Curator
National Museum of American History

Stephanie Anastasopoulos, M.Ed.
TOSA, STREAM Integration
Solana Beach School District

Publishing Credits

Rachelle Cracchiolo, M.S.Ed., *Publisher*
Conni Medina, M.A.Ed., *Managing Editor*
Diana Kenney, M.A.Ed., NBCT, *Content Director*
Véronique Bos, *Creative Director*
Robin Erickson, *Art Director*
Michelle Jovin, M.A., *Associate Editor*
Mindy Duits, *Senior Graphic Designer*
Smithsonian Science Education Center

Image Credits: p.5 (top) Lanmas/Alamy; p.5 (middle) Vatican Apostolic Library, The Yorck Project; p.5 (bottom) © Smithsonian; p.8 (top) SPL/Science Source; p.8 (bottom) SSPL/Getty Images; p.12 (left) Wetwebwork/Flickr; p.12 (right), p.19 (top) MediaPunch Inc./Alamy; p.13 (bottom) PhilipR/Shutterstock; p.14 United States Patent and Trademark Office; p.15 (right) Philip Pilosian/Shutterstock; p.16 (left) Pictorial Press Ltd/Alamy; pp.16–17 Philippe Gras/Le Pictorium/Newscom; p.18 (left) Frank Forcino/NameFace/Sipa USA/Newscom; pp.18–19 Splash News/Alamy; p.19 (bottom) Robert LeSieur/Reuters/Newscom; pp.20–21 Nick_Nick/Shutterstock; p.21 (top left) courtesy Raymond Boyd; p.21 (top right) Dydric [Creative Commons BY-SA 2.5]; p.22 courtesy Andy Cavatorta; p.24 Photo by Ryan Scott, courtesy of the Drexel ExCITe Center; p.25 (top) courtesy of the Drexel ExCITe Center; p.25 (bottom) courtesy of the Drexel ExCITe Center, drawing by Peter English and Jeff Gregorio; p.26 Kul Bhatia/Science Source; p.32 (left) Bruce Mars; all other images from iStock and/or Shutterstock.

Library of Congress Cataloging-in-Publication Data

Names: Urquhart, Kristina Mercedes, author.
Title: Making music with magnets / Kristina Mercedes Urquhart.
Description: Huntington Beach, CA : Teacher Created Materials, [2019] |
   Includes index. |
Identifiers: LCCN 2018022127 (print) | LCCN 2018022872 (ebook) | ISBN
   9781493869534 (E-book) | ISBN 9781493867134 (pbk.)
Subjects: LCSH: Electric guitar--Juvenile literature.
Classification: LCC ML1015.G9 (ebook) | LCC ML1015.G9 U77 2019 (print)
| DDC
   787.87/19--dc23
LC record available at https://lccn.loc.gov/2018022127

Teacher Created Materials

5301 Oceanus Drive
Huntington Beach, CA 92649-1030
www.tcmpub.com
ISBN 978-1-4938-6713-4

Table of Contents

Origin Story

The guitar is one of the most widely used instruments in the world. You may think of it as a modern invention, but the first guitar-like instruments date back thousands of years! They have changed a lot since then, but whatever they look like, they're made to play music.

The oldest ancestors of the modern guitar were ancient stringed instruments. The *tanbur* was one such stringed instrument. The Egyptian tanbur dates back four thousand years and looks similar to a modern guitar. It has a long, straight neck, a pear-shaped body, and strings across a soundboard. In ancient times, the strings were made from the guts of animals, such as cows and cats.

Hundreds of years later, a group of Muslims brought their own stringed instrument, called an *oud*, to Spain. The oud was shorter and rounder than most tanburs. From the oud came the Spanish *guitarra*. The guitarra is the earliest ancestor of the modern guitar. It soon spread to France, England, and Germany. From there it changed many times over the years and continued to spread around the world.

18th century engraving of a man playing a stringed instrument

13th century illumination of a man playing an oud

Ancient Egyptian wall paintings show people playing tanburs together in groups. These paintings are more than 3,500 years old!

Turn Up the Volume

For a long time, people were happy with guitar music just as it was. However, some musicians thought guitars were too quiet. They couldn't be heard over trumpets, drums, and pianos. They needed to be louder!

Making Music

Today, the two most common types of guitar are **acoustic** and electric. They look similar from the outside. The top of both guitars is called the head. The head holds the strings and has tuning pegs, which loosen or tighten the strings. Connected to the head is the fingerboard of the guitar. The fingerboard is where the strings are located. On the fingerboard are different frets, which are metal strips. Artists can use a finger to hold the string down on one of the frets, which will change the **pitch** of the note. This allows the guitarist to play many musical notes.

Acoustic and electric guitars may look similar. However, the way they make music is very different. Acoustic guitars have hollow bodies with holes in the middle, appropriately called sound holes. First, a musician plucks the strings. Then, the vibrations from those strings travel down to the sound hole. The vibrating hollow hole makes the air inside vibrate, which makes sounds.

inside an acoustic guitar

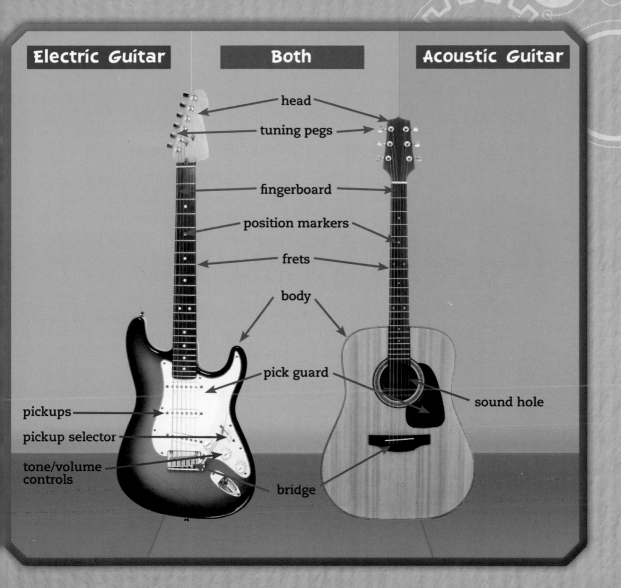

Electric Guitar | **Both** | **Acoustic Guitar**

- head
- tuning pegs
- fingerboard
- position markers
- frets
- body
- pick guard
- sound hole
- pickups
- pickup selector
- tone/volume controls
- bridge

TECHNOLOGY

Catgut Your Tongue?

Today's acoustic guitars use plastic nylon for their strings, but ancient guitarists used natural materials to create their strings. The earliest cords were made from animal intestines and were called catgut. Sometimes called "gut" for short, these strings made a rich, warm sound.

Electric guitars are different. They use **electromagnets** to make sound. Electromagnets are made from **conductive** wire and metal. First, a piece of metal wire is wrapped around a piece of metal. Then, electricity is added. This creates the electromagnet. Electromagnets are different from normal magnets. Magnets do not need a power source; electromagnets do. When the power is on, the electromagnet is on. When it is off, so is the electromagnet.

William Sturgeon made the first electromagnet. He was a British engineer. While he was in the army, he went to Newfoundland. While there, he watched thunder in the sky. These storms made him want to learn more about electricity. How did it work? What could he learn from it?

When Sturgeon got home, he started working with magnets and electricity. At first, he just passed electricity through coils of wire to create a **magnetic field**. In 1825, Sturgeon had an idea. He wrapped wire around a piece of metal. Then, he added electricity. His magnet was much stronger than it was before. He did not know that his work would impact the world of music!

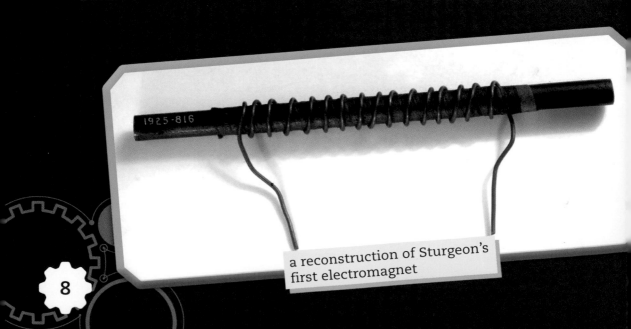

1925-816

a reconstruction of Sturgeon's first electromagnet

A doctor prepares a patient for an MRI.

Electromagnets can be found in telephones, electric motors, MRI machines, and earphones.

Electric guitars rely on Sturgeon's invention. Without electromagnets, electric guitars would not make loud sounds. People hear sounds from acoustic guitars because they are hollow and have sound holes. But electric guitars aren't hollow and don't have sound holes. Instead, they need a power source to make sound.

For electric guitars, the power source comes from **amplifiers**, or amps. When an amp is turned on, the flow of electricity from the amp does two things. First, it travels to a piece of wire-wrapped metal. This part is called the pickup, and it acts as an electromagnet. Second, it creates a magnetic field around the metal strings on the fingerboard. When the strings are plucked, they vibrate. Those vibrations travel down to the pickup. The pickup then **converts** the vibrations from the strings into an electric current. The current passes through a wire to the amp. The amp projects the loud sounds from the guitar. It may seem like a long and complex process. But all of that happens faster than it takes to blink!

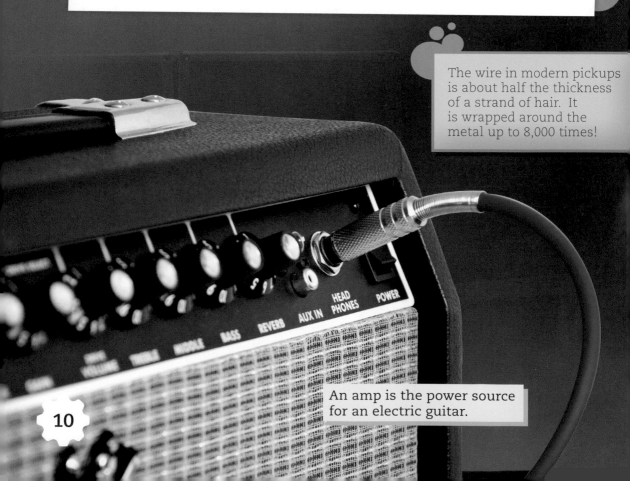

The wire in modern pickups is about half the thickness of a strand of hair. It is wrapped around the metal up to 8,000 times!

An amp is the power source for an electric guitar.

Amped Up

The basis of an electromagnet is a piece of metal (usually iron) wrapped in wire. The wire is usually copper. Alone, these two objects are quiet. But when you add electricity, they come to life! When a current is added, a magnetic field forms around the wire. This turns the metal into a magnet while the electricity is on. Turn off the current, and you turn off the magnet!

guitar string

magnetic field

vibrations from string

amp

wire-wrapped metal (electromagnet)

speaker

diagram of wiring in an electric guitar

The Birth of the Electric Guitar

Electric guitars are a common sight today. Go to a concert, and there will probably be a musician rocking out with an electric guitar. But that was not always the case. In fact, electric guitars are a relatively recent sight.

The first electric guitar was invented in 1931. It was created by a man named George Beauchamp (BEE-chuhm). He wanted to make acoustic guitars louder. His finished project was nicknamed the Frying Pan because of its round body and long neck. It looked just like a frying pan! The Frying Pan was an electric version of an acoustic guitar—a lap steel guitar. Musicians laid lap steel guitars on their laps and played by plucking the strings. Moving a steel rod along the strings changed the pitch of the notes. At the base of the strings, there were pickups shaped like horseshoes. They converted the vibrations to electric currents, which were amplified and played through speakers.

The Frying Pan made a unique sound and quickly became popular in Hawaiian music. It had a twang that can still be heard today. Soon, other guitar companies started making electric guitars just like it. The Frying Pan's special sound influenced certain types of music, such as bluegrass and big band.

Beauchamp's first Frying Pan guitar

Bluegrass is named after one of its founders, Bill Monroe. Monroe named his band the Blue Grass Boys after his home state of Kentucky (the Bluegrass State).

A guitarist slides a steel rod across the strings of a lap steel guitar.

A bluegrass band plays on a street in St. Louis, Missouri.

Beauchamp first sold the Frying Pan in 1932. He applied for a **patent** two years later. But his patent was not awarded for another three years. In that time, other companies used his model to make their own electric guitars. Soon, there were new styles for people to choose from.

Electric guitars started being used in new **genres**. They were not just in Hawaiian music anymore. This was the music scene in the 1940s that Leo Fender found himself in. Fender was a radio repairman. Over the years, he heard more and more electric guitars on the radio. Fender thought the electric guitar was starting to take off. So in 1946, Fender founded his own guitar company.

Beauchamp's patent

The first Fender guitar was built in 1951. It was called the Fender Telecaster. Some people thought it was too simple. One of those people was Ted McCarty—the president of the guitar company Gibson. McCarty called the Telecaster a "plank guitar." McCarty thought Fender's guitar lacked **craftsmanship**. These comments sparked a rivalry between Fender and Gibson. Both worked to make the best guitars.

Telecaster with two pickups

Stratocaster with three pickups

Higher Than Ever

After the Telecaster, Fender built the Stratocaster (STRA-tuh-kas-tuhr). It was the first guitar to have three pickups instead of two. That extra pickup could pick up more vibrations, which allowed for more **tones**. The Stratocaster had a new "tremolo" system too. This device let artists raise and lower the pitch of their strings. These new designs gave artists more control than ever over their music.

Electric Guitars Take Over

The feud between Fender and Gibson turned out to be a good thing. It helped them create some of the most **versatile** guitars in the world. This meant their guitars could do more than just play standard notes. Musicians could now change the tones, volumes, and pitches of their notes too. They could also use accessories to change the sounds of the guitars. Guitarists were creative and playful. They found many ways to make new sounds with their guitars.

The rise of rock 'n' roll music in the 1950s and '60s led to new techniques. Guitarists learned they could change the sound by standing closer to or farther from their amps. Some used different items to pluck their strings, such as their fingernails or new styles of **picks**. And all the while, Fender's Stratocaster and Gibson's Les Paul guitars were leading the pack as two of the most popular guitars available.

In 1948, musician Les Paul shattered his elbow in a car accident. Paul had his arm **set** at an angle so that he could still play the guitar. Four years later, he invented the Gibson Les Paul guitar.

16

Jimi Hendrix was one of the most popular electric guitarists in the world in the 1960s.

The rock 'n' roll craze gave way to heavy metal in the 1970s and '80s. Heavy metal music has a strong focus on electric guitar sounds. Artists wanted to be able to make new sounds to match the mood of the genre. Soon, new equipment became available. Devices, such as the wah-wah pedal, helped guitarists create new sounds.

Songs now featured long guitar solos. The electric guitarist had quickly become one of the most important players in a band. Heavy guitar riffs were common and would last for minutes at a time. Guitarists, such as Eddie Van Halen and Carlos Santana, were becoming celebrities. And heavy metal bands, such as Aerosmith and Guns N' Roses, were household names.

Heavy metal gave way to grunge music in the '90s. Nirvana and Pearl Jam were two leaders of the genre. They mixed new guitar sounds with heartfelt lyrics. The electric guitar was still a key part of the band. But it was now being used to make people experience heartache.

Lead singer of Nirvana, Kurt Cobain, performs in 1993.

Lead singer of Pearl Jam, Eddie Vedder, performs in 2016.

Guns N' Roses performs in 1988.

Making His Own

Van Halen wasn't happy with electric guitars in the '70s. So he combined parts from old Fender and Gibson guitars. Van Halen's fans called his new guitar the "Frankenstein." He painted it in a unique black-and-white striped pattern to make it stand out. But he saw other people copying his paint job, so he repainted it a bright red color. Van Halen's red Frankenstein is still one of the most recognizable guitars of all time.

Van Halen holds a replica of his Frankenstein guitar.

Recently, electric guitars have seen a drop in sales with the rise of new genres. Folk music relies on acoustic guitars. Hip-hop music focuses more on record scratching than loud guitars. And pop and electronic dance music (EDM) are based in electronic sounds. For those genres, the more it sounds like a computer the better.

However, all is not lost for electric guitars. They have found a new home in different places. **Orchestras** have begun using electric guitarists in their concerts. Online stars are playing their own versions of classical music. You can now hear Bach and Mozart songs with an electric guitar twist.

Guitar schools have also seen a rise in young players. These schools teach beginners how to play. Most of the songs they teach are rock songs from the '60s and '70s. But they also teach players newer songs. It is now common to hear songs from Taylor Swift, Ed Sheeran, and Twenty One Pilots blasting out of electric guitar schools.

An electric guitarist performs in an Italian orchestra in 2016.

Turntables like this one by Technics use electromagnets to amplify sounds.

Run-DMC members Darryl "DMC" McDaniels and Joseph "Run" Simmons are famous for their rapping and their record scratching on turntables.

Synthesizers were popular in the '60s, but they are used in modern EDM music too. Early versions used electromagnets to make their sounds.

early synthesizer

It's Electric

Music will likely always have a place for electric guitars. But even if it doesn't, there are other instruments that can make music with magnets. People are using old instruments in new ways. Some people are even making their own instruments.

Designer Andy Cavatorta made his own instrument, which he calls the Overtone Harp. He wanted to make something that had never been done before. And he did! The Overtone Harp is played as both a piano and a harp.

The Overtone Harp works in the opposite way of the electric guitar. With electric guitars, vibrations on the strings create electric currents in the electromagnets. In the Harp, the electromagnets create their own currents, which vibrate the strings. By turning the electricity on, the electromagnet pulls the Harp's strings. Turning it off lets the strings go. Doing this over and over produces big sounds.

The Overtone Harp is meant to be played by two people. One person plucks, strums, taps, or hammers the strings. The second person plays a keyboard connected to electromagnets. The magnets are attached to a soundboard. When the two players play together, they create layers of sound.

Cavatorta's Overtone Harp

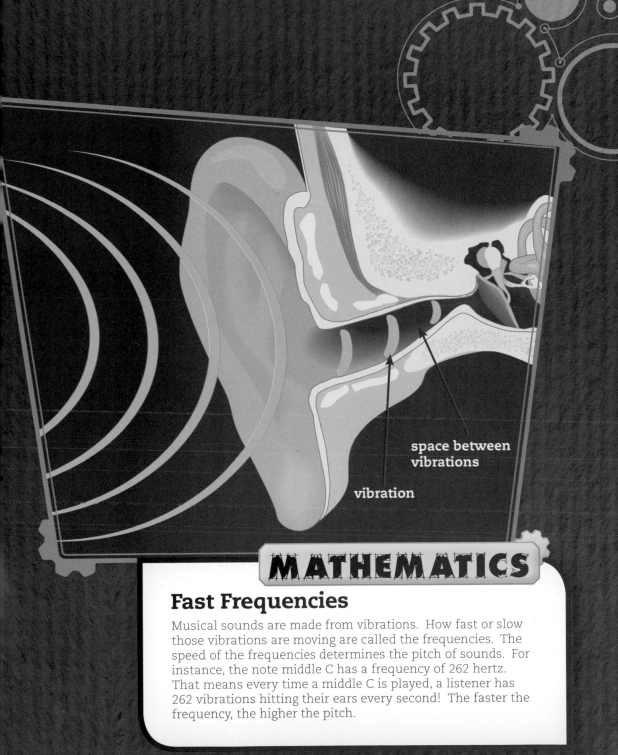

space between
vibrations

vibration

MATHEMATICS

Fast Frequencies

Musical sounds are made from vibrations. How fast or slow
those vibrations are moving are called the frequencies. The
speed of the frequencies determines the pitch of sounds. For
instance, the note middle C has a frequency of 262 hertz.
That means every time a middle C is played, a listener has
262 vibrations hitting their ears every second! The faster the
frequency, the higher the pitch.

Another magnetic instrument is Drumhenge. It looks like a group of regular drums, but these drums are far from normal! Usually, a drummer hits a drumhead with a drumstick. The vibrations of the drumhead produce sound waves in the air. Drumhenge works differently. Each of the 16 drumheads has a piece of steel foil and an electromagnet. When a signal is sent to the electromagnet, the drumhead vibrates. The vibrations create different pitches. All 16 drumheads combine to make one huge instrument.

Drumhenge artists can control the pitch of the drums with digital controllers. They can choose how many drums they want to play. But that is not all. Drumhenge is also adjustable. An artist can choose which notes they want the drums to play. Or, they can play a different instrument, such as a saxophone. Drumhenge will listen and analyze the music it hears. It will then play in harmony with the new instrument. That lets an artist play two instruments at once!

The Drumhenge team plays different instruments while Drumhenge plays along.

Drumhenge was made at the ExCITe Center of Drexel University by Peter English and Jeff Gregorio. They wanted to see how music, technology, and **interactivity** worked together.

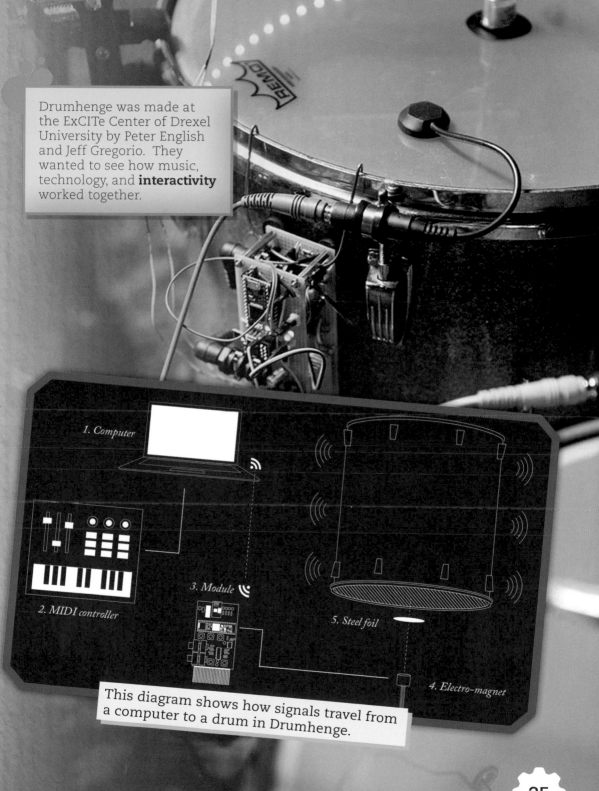

1. Computer

2. MIDI controller

3. Module

4. Electro-magnet

5. Steel foil

This diagram shows how signals travel from a computer to a drum in Drumhenge.

A New Sound

Electromagnets have played a powerful role in music. Without them, we would not have some of the great songs we have today. In particular, we would not have electric guitars. Without electric guitars, decades' worth of music would not be the same.

The electric guitar was born because of new technology. But how will technology change music in the future? Today, there are computer programs that make hundreds of sounds. Some scientists think that may be a bad thing. They say that listening to computer-created music is changing our brains. They believe this music is too perfect. Our brains like music that is **unpredictable**. Otherwise, we can guess what is going to happen next in a song. Studies show that our brains may find that boring.

So how can we keep things interesting? Go to concerts and see the unpredictable side of live music. Or invent new ways to use magnets to make sounds. You never know—you may influence the future of music!

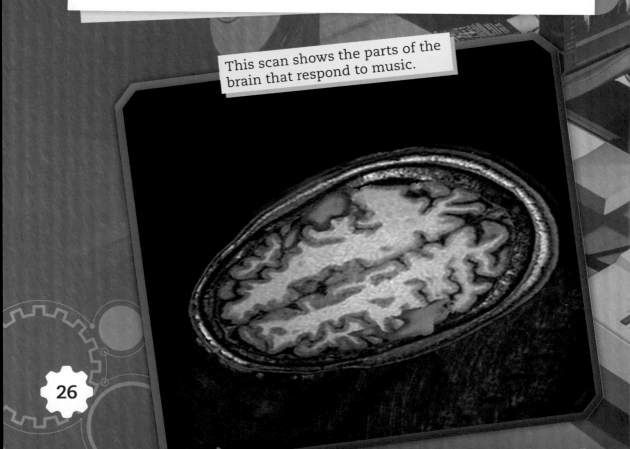

This scan shows the parts of the brain that respond to music.

People have been studying the brain for hundreds of years. One study found that when guitarists play a duet, their brain waves **synchronize** with each other!

27

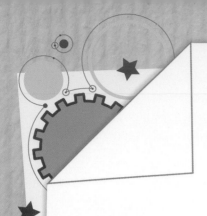

STEAM CHALLENGE

Define the Problem

Imagine you are a music teacher planning to teach your class about pitch. Your idea is to demonstrate the concept with simple materials. For the lesson, you must design and build an instrument that plays four different pitches.

Constraints: You may only use four types of materials to build the instrument.

Criteria: Your instrument must play four distinct pitches.

1. Research and Brainstorm

What are pitches? How can electric guitarists change pitches? How did the creation of the electric guitar change the future of music?

2. Design and Build

Sketch your instrument design. What purpose will each part serve? What materials will work best? Build the model.

3. Test and Improve

Have a friend listen as you play your instrument. Did they hear four different pitches? How can you improve it? Modify your design and try again.

4. Reflect and Share

How do different materials affect pitch? How can you produce a louder sound? Can you modify your instrument to add more pitches? Why don't you need a power source to hear your instrument's sounds?

Glossary

acoustic—refers to an instrument that does not have an electronic system for amplifying notes

amplifiers—devices that make sounds played through electronic systems sound louder

conductive—able to allow the flow of electricity

converts—changes something from one form to another so it can be used in a different way

craftsmanship—work that is done with great skill

electromagnets—metals that become magnetic when electrical currents are passed through or near them

genres—particular categories or types of art forms

interactivity—refers to a system that responds to the actions of a user

lyrics—the words in songs

magnetic field—an invisible region around a magnetic object which influences other magnetic objects around it

orchestras—groups of musicians who are led by a conductor and play usually classical music together

patent—an official guarantee for an inventor to be the only one to make, use, and sell their invention

picks—thin, small pieces of plastic or metal that are used to play the strings on some instruments

pitch—how high or low a sound is, determined by the frequency of the sound; usually referred to as "deep" or "shrill" sounds

riffs—short, usually repeated patterns of notes in songs

set—put into a certain position

synchronize—happen at the same time and speed

tones—sounds that happen at particular pitches and volumes

unpredictable—behaving in a way that is hard to predict or expect

versatile—capable of doing many different things or having many different uses

Index

CAREER ADVICE
from Smithsonian

Do you want to make music?
Here are some tips to get you started.

"Music can be life-changing and fun. The diversity of people, histories, and cultures has led to a rich variety of sounds, styles, and genres. I am fortunate to live and work with music from around the world every day. Learn to play an instrument: piano, guitar, or even spoons. Music is everywhere so stop and listen to all the sounds around you." —*Huib Schippers, Director of Smithsonian Folkways Recordings*

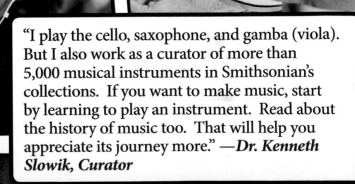

"I play the cello, saxophone, and gamba (viola). But I also work as a curator of more than 5,000 musical instruments in Smithsonian's collections. If you want to make music, start by learning to play an instrument. Read about the history of music too. That will help you appreciate its journey more." —*Dr. Kenneth Slowik, Curator*